NEVER SHALL I FORGET

by
Joseph Winteringham

Foreword by
Jane Cooper

Published by Threepeppers Publishing

Copyright © 2020 Jane Cooper
Copyright © 2020 Threepeppers Publishing

Jane Cooper has asserted her right under the Copyright, Designs and Patents Act, 1988, to be identified as the author of this work.

All rights reserved. No part of this book shall be reproduced, stored in a retrieval system, or transmitted by any means – electronic, mechanical, photocopying, recording, or otherwise – without written permission from the author and the publisher.

1st Edition – November 2020

ISBN: 9781999326876

Cover:
Joseph Winteringham's Military Achievements: (*from left*) Queen Victoria Sudan; Khedives Sudan; Queen Victoria South Africa with clasps for Transvaal, Paardenberg, Relief of Kimberley, Modder River, Belmont; King Edward VII South Africa with clasps for South Africa 1901 & 1902; 1914/15 Star medal; British War for service in World War One; Allied Victory with oak leaf for "Mentioned in Dispatches"

Photo © Jane Cooper

www.3peppers.co.uk

To Joseph and Clifford

Foreword

by Jane Cooper (née Winteringham)

I have to confess that we are very lucky to have this little book, and certainly should not have done had it not been for my good friend and neighbour Charlotte, who was helping me sort some of my father's multitude of paperwork and old letters at the time.

After my own father died this little book was in a battered old case along with a lot of electrical training notes. I initially put it on the recycling pile along with the notes, assuming it to be more of the same. It was only when my friend picked it up and started reading the first page aloud that we realised what a treasure we had.

What followed was a magical evening getting to know my grandfather for the first time, since he had died 24 years before I was born. It was almost as though he was speaking directly to me from all those years ago. I remember my father telling me how strict Joseph had been with his children. It was refreshing to learn that as a child Joseph himself had been naughty and wilful and must have driven his eldest sister to distraction at times.

I felt at that point that I had several cousins who would be interested to read it, and noting that the book was in quite a fragile state decided that I should really transcribe the whole thing, just as Grandad Joseph had written it, complete with spelling mistakes and lack of punctuation.

It appears that the early life memoirs were written not long before Joseph died in 1932, perhaps when he became unwell. There are no dates or ages mentioned in the book, but I have since found a record of his brother William on a list of fishing apprentices in Grimsby where he was sent for some "misdemeanour"! I wonder to this day what it was he did that was so awful, but Joseph does not tell us. The section about his travels and work in what is now Namibia appear to have been written contemporaneously as a diary.

Thanks must go to my husband Ken, for reading it out loud for me to type, when my will to continue was flagging.

A big thank you also goes to my cousin Carol Winteringham for suggesting the idea and her son David Tripepi for turning this diary into a book you can read and enjoy.

Note from the Publisher

This book is a direct copy of the original documents, which have been transcribed as they were found. A series of question marks and words in parentheses have been added where the text was perhaps illegible or unclear, and assumptions may have been drawn on what was written. The text has not been altered, in order to maintain the writing style and spirit of Joseph Winteringham, including some misspellings like the word "Pyramids". In a few instances, punctuation and some English possessive forms have been added to simplify the reading.

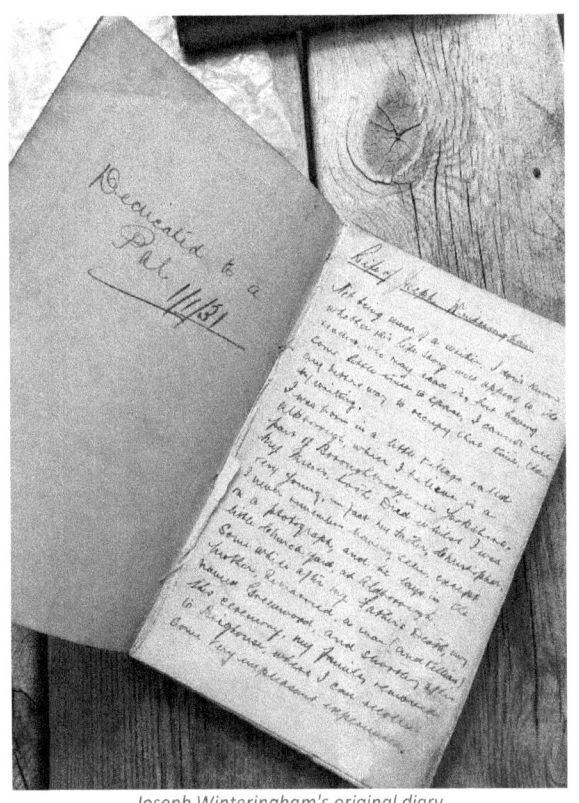

Joseph Winteringham's original diary

The Early Life of Joseph Winteringham (1879-1905)

Transcribed from his notebook by his granddaughter Jane Cooper (née Winteringham)

Dedicated to a Pal 1/1/31

Not being much of a writer, I don't know whether this life story will appeal to the readers, who may read it, but having some little time to spare, I cannot see any other time to occupy the time, than by writing.

I was born in a little village called Aldborough, which I believe is a part of Boroughbridge in Yorkshire. My parents both died whilst I was very young, in fact my father, Christopher, I never remember having seen, except in a photograph, and he lays in the little churchyard at Aldborough.

Some while after my father's death, my mother remarried, a man (and villain) named Greenwood, and shortly after this ceremony, my family removed to Brighouse, where I can recollect some very unpleasant experiences.

Being quite a youngster when we removed to Brighouse, I cannot recall much of my early days in Boroughbridge and my memory will only carry me back to Brighouse, where I first started to go to school.

At that time I remember we lived as far as I can recall, as a happy family, and I understand from my brothers and sisters, that we had a very large family, thirteen in number, of which I was the youngest.

So far as I can remember, our house was situated, between two others, and quite close to the riverbank (which I suppose would be the Leeds-Liverpool Canal), in a quiet country lane.

Not very far distant was a factory of some kind, where my stepfather and eldest brother worked and before I began school, it was a duty of mine to take their dinners at midday.

Recalling the fact that I was a meal carrier, brings back to my memory, the first hiding I ever had at the hands of a brute, (which I always called the man who married and ill-treated my mother).

It happened in this way, I was told one day as usual to carry dinner to the works, and as I had to always wait for the empty basket, I played about on some frozen ground near by, until I could collect the empties and go home.

On my way home, I felt a little hungry, so I looked in the basket to see if there was a crust of bread left. That was the cause of my hiding with the buckle end of a belt, which I shall never forget, and I have often prayed to meet Mr Greenwood, and pay him back, but it was never my luck. Well, to come back to the basket, on searching I found a sandwich made of bread and mustard, (the meat had been taken out), and I ate this during my walk home.

When my stepfather returned at night, the first thing he should ask for, was the bread which he had left from dinner, why he should want this I don't know, because my mother kept a good table, and there was plenty of food prepared for him.

Anyhow, mother said the basket was empty when I brought it home, and I thought, in my childish mind that I should speak up, so I said I felt hungry when I was on my way home, and I eat it.

That started the war between me and that brute.

That Devil pulled off my collar, and although, I can see now, my mother trying to protect me, I got a hiding that I swore in my childish way, I would never allow anyone else to give me as long as I lived.

Shortly after this incident, I was thought old enough to go to school, and one morning in middle winter, I can now picture my mother, trudging me along over the two miles of frozen ground to the school, where I was taken as a scholar, with my other brothers and sisters.

I can't say that I took too kindly to school, and one incident in my early school days turned me against school and teaching of any kind. Never shall I forget the day, that I and my brother, who was two years older than I was, set off to school, with our dinners under our arms, swinging along the road, which was very frosty. On our way we had to pass a sheet of water, which was frozen over, and we of course, could not resist the temptation to have a few slides.

We were enjoying ourselves immensely, and quite ignorant of the time, until we began to feel rather hungry, and then it was, that we realised that we were what they called playing truant. Anyhow, we stayed on the ice until my sisters were coming home from school, and then to return home. We never dreamt that we had committed an awful offence, and of course said nothing to anyone.

The next day we went to school like good boys, but the teacher wanted to know where my brother was the day before, but I, being so young, I was not asked anything.

On school being over at the end of the day, the teacher called my brother to him, and wrote on his slate, (we carried slates to school then), a message to my mother to explain his absence on the previous day. That is the time we were afraid, not knowing what to do, as we dare not tell mother, so between us we wrote and excuse to the teacher. The teacher knowing full well that it was not mother's writing, sent a letter for mother to come to school on the next day.

Had either my brother or myself known we should cause her to have to walk three or four miles to school, we should never have done what we did, but child-like, how could we have known we were going to cause mother to have an anxious time.

Well, Mother came to the school the next morning, and had an interview with the teacher, but little did I know what that interview meant to me.

On my return from school, cold and hungry, I was met by mother, who told me to take off my coat, and she gave me a good thrashing with a strap, which was kept for the purpose, and then I was sent to bed without tea or anything. That was not for playing truant, but for telling a falsehood.

But the worst had still to come from my stepfather.

It must have been very late at night when he returned home, as I think we were all in bed, and with the exception of myself, they were hard and fast asleep, but poor me, I could not sleep from hunger and a broken heart, and I lay sobbing in bed, until I heard the windows on the roof open, and saw a man getting in, and did not know who it was until he spoke and then I knew it was my stepfather, who had been locked out, and had got a ladder, of which there was an abundance in the yard behind, and he had climbed on the roof, opened the window, and slid down the iron rod, which holds the attic window open.

He dropped on my bed, and then I heard him go to his own bedroom, and straight start talking to mother.

The next I heard, was them both having words, and he saying he would give me a good hiding again. Mother tried to persuade not to, as she said I had had quite enough, but as I know now, he must have been drinking, and was determined to teach me a lesson, then he came into my bedroom, and I got it again, and then I heard him ask for a piece of string to pull my tongue out. I was not afraid of the strap, but I was terribly afraid he would carry out his threat, but he eventually went off to bed, leaving me with a much more broken heart. Oh if I could only have met that man, when I got to manhood.

After this, things went very smoothly so far as I was concerned, until a few months later, I was left an orphan.

It happened this way, my mother one night went to a concert, so I am told, at the Town Hall, (in) Brighouse, and (when) she returned home, she had caught a chill, from which she never recovered, but, I am told, being too young to understand, that her death was hastened, by her husband coming home one night, tipsy I suppose, and pulling the bed about the room, that of course made mother worse, and a few days after, she was gone.

Never shall I forget the day, when the funeral took place.

I remember quite well, how I sat on the fence opposite our house, watching for the horses and carriage, in which I was going to have a ride. I can even now, so many years ago, see myself sitting on the fence, eating plenty of finger biscuits, which were, I believe, very much in demand in those days.

We did not stay in Brighouse very long after mothers funeral, and then we removed to Leeds, and then we were separated for a time. How long we were apart, I don't quite remember, but I do know, that I was put in charge of one of my fathers brothers named William, who then lived in the West Street district.

I have quite a good recollection of this, because, on arrival at my uncle's home, I had to have a bath, as we had had a long journey, and the day was cold and dark.

I well remember, that after having a bath, the bath was put under the table, whilst we were having tea, and I being rather tired, rested my feet on the edge of the bath.

Not being content with this, or it may have been forgetfulness , in any case before I knew what had happened the bath, which was full of water, came over, and of course the kitchen was soon flooded, and consequently I was soon upstairs to bed, after a good spanking.

Well, things went on very smoothly after this accident, and then the family was again united, my eldest sister having got a house, where we could all live together.

I begin School

At this time, I was considered old enough to begin to become educated, and I was sent to a school quite close to our home.

After going to school for a few week, things began to change for us. In the first place, my sisters began leaving home to go into service[1], and in a very short time, there was only my oldest sister and us three lads left in the house.

Not long after this, my eldest brother, Bill, misconducted himself and was sent on a fishing smack at Grimsby.

Then it was my sister, decided to remove into a smaller house, which we eventually did, and this removal caused me to walk much further to school, than I had to do before.

School did not appeal to me in those days, and I am afraid, I played more truant, than I attended school.

I very well remember, that somewhere in the Balm Road district, there was a factory known to us as the old silk mill, and in a field behind the mill, was a kind of stream, where the warm water

---

[1] Publisher's Note: as standards of social decorum for the upper classes increased in the later Victorian period, the need for domestic servants in Victorian England increased as well

was run out of the mill, and several of us youngsters, instead of going to school, would take a holiday and go off bathing.

Dozens, ah, I could say hundreds of times, the School Board Bobby, as we called him then, would come down to the old mill, to catch us, but he never could do, because we always had one of us lads on the look out for him. I remember one day, I decided I would go to school and turn good, and that morning found me in my place in the classroom, but I was not allowed to remain there long. I had been sat for a little while, and thought that I was doing my lessons very well, and paying attention to my teacher, when the headmaster (Mr Woods) came into the room, and called me out, and asked me where I had been for several days, and not being used to telling lies, I told him that I had been swimming at the silk mill in Hunslet.

He took me to his room and gave me a good talking, to which I think I should have taken notice of, had he let it stop at that, but when he had had his say, he gave me a good caning, and locked me in a room when all the others had gone out to play, and also when the class were dismissed to go home for dinner.

This was rather too much for my rebellious spirit, and no sooner had the door been locked on me, then I was out of the window, and school did not see me again for some days.

Eventually after many years of hardships I, on my twelve birthday, commenced to earn my own living.

I Start to Work

Never shall I forget the Monday morning when I set off, with a nice clean white apron on, to work as a grocer's errand boy, little thinking that I should have to all my life, up to now.

My work was to try and keep the shop clean, both inside and outside, to wash currants and raisins and to run errands. Many a time I had to go quite long distances with groceries in a basket, and now when I recall the time, I am afraid that boy like, I took up too much of my master's time delivering the goods. Things ran very smoothly all week and, it would be hard to find a more proud boy in the land, when on the Saturday night, I took home my first hard earned money, to the amount of four shillings.

My wage, I gave to my sister, who if I remember right, gave me the magnificent sum of twopence all for myself.

I had not been working many weeks when through a misunderstanding I lost my job.

It happened, this way. Whilst washing currants and raisins, I got into the habit of putting some of the fruit into my mouth, and then some into my pocket, to eat when I was out on my errands.

One day my master said, his son would go with me on an errand, for company. To this I did not object, as I was rather fond of the boy, but the scamp, put me away to his father when we returned.

Never thinking that I was doing wrong, whilst out, but I shared eating the raisins which I had in my pockets, and foolish lad I was, I gave some to the lad who was with me. Of course when we got back to the shop, the boy told his father that I had a pocket full of raisins, and that I had given him some to eat.

Naturally I was called to my master, who gave me a good talking to, and told me, as I understand now, I was dismissed. I did not allow the grass to grow under my feet, because of this incident, for on the following morning, I set off at five o'clock to look for work.

Work in those days was not hard to get, and after trying several places without any luck, I was making my way home, hungry tired and cold, when what should I see in front of me, but "Notice Boy Wanted" at Lightmans, up the yard.

I did not stop to look twice, but went up the yard like a shot, and after a little while, I was seen by the man who was the master, because after a little talk I was told I could start right away.

Oh, what joy I off with my coat and was taken to a man, who was doing something with large pieces of wood, and told he would be my boss for the time being.

The place where I had started to work, was a furniture manufactory, and the man was a wood turner, and turning the pieces of wood into chair and table legs.

Eventually, twelve noon came, and hearing a whistle blowing I enquired what it was, and I was told to clear off for my dinner, and be back in an hour's time.

I had a long way to go home to let my sister know, and to my surprise she had just got some oven cakes out of the oven. Never shall I forget that midday, when I walked into the house, and I don't think a grown man could have given an order for dinner better than I did. Of course for my authority I got my ears boxed, but when I explained, that I had to be back at work at one o'clock, (I should have one this first!) I was soon given some dinner, which consisted of new cake & fried bacon, but never did I enjoy a meal better than this one.

I did not stay long at this work, as a friend of mine, asked me to try and get a job where he was working, and after a few days I was successful in getting work in Hardings in Globe Road.

This work for a boy was rather hard, because I had to stand on a high platform and to feed a machine with long steel rods, which , when they had passed through the machine, they came out with sharpened points, and then they turned round to do the same with the other end, and then it was that the hard work came on. When both ends of the rods had been ground down, I had to keep on feeding the machine with the rods handed up to me by the boss, and it was absolutely necessary to keep them quite level, or they would cause a jam in the wheel, and many's the time I would have liked to cry out in pain, as I forced, with cut and bleeding hands, the rods into their positions.

I stayed at the work for quite a long time, until certain events happened, which caused me, in my boyish way, to change my mind.

First of all my second eldest brother was sent away to a school for some misconduct, which I did not understand then, so I don't think I will mention it again, and I and my sister were left by our two selfs. Not long after this my sister, Olie, and the one of my sisters who was in service came to look after the house, and then it was that we then removed into a house that was to prove very memorable to me.

This sister eventually got work at a clothiers near to where I was working, and between us we got on very well together, and one day, I was about 14 years old then I believe, I thought I would like to learn a trade, and I was fortunate to get a job at Blasseys in Lady Lane.

This kind of work appealed to me very much, and I took so much interest in my work that I was very soon put on a bench by myself, and from that time I was known as a boot riveter, and I could at that time, earn between twelve and fourteen shillings a week, which I handed over to my sister, who gave me sixpence back for myself, which I thought was very good for a boy.

As I write this, I wonder what a boy of my age (then) would think if he only got sixpence pocket money. Time went on until I got dissatisfied with my money, and not being able to persuade my masters that I thought I was worth more, I tried to find a new shop, which after a few days, I did, and I commenced work at Midgley[2] boot manufactory in Swinegate.

It was whilst working here, that I had my first taste of being a prisoner in a court of law. I quite well remember, one day during the dinner hour, I and some more boys, made a ball with some paper, and went into the street to play football. The game had not been long in progress, before a man in blue came upon the scene, and I was the unlucky one to be caught, and I had to appear at

---

[2] Publisher's Note: what became known later as A. W. Midgley & Sons Ltd., a company still in operation in the Leeds area

the Town Hall before a magistrate, and for that my first and last appearance as a prisoner in an English court, I was fined one shilling.

Shortly after this, something happened which caused me to turn round all together, and change my view of life. At this time my eldest brother, who I learned had got on very well on the fishing smack, came over from Grimsby. I afterwards heard that he had got married and of course, his wife came with him.

I remember that on that occasion, I asked him to take me back to Grimsby with him, and get me on to a fishing smack. I had a great fancy for the sea in those days, but try as I would, my brother refused to take me back, and instead he took my cousin, who was about my own age.

The next day I went to work as usual, and worked hard, as I was determined to get some money, and my way alone.

Eventually night time came, and I started my walk home, eager for some tea, but judge to my surprise when I arrived home, to find myself locked out.

At that time we lived next door to my sister's fiancee, so I went there to enquire, what was wrong, and I was told, that my brother and wife, and my sister and her young man, had gone for a day trip to Boroughbridge, and even then when I was so young, I realised that I had been snubbed, and being in the house alone, I felt that I had been absolutely left out in the cold, and no-one to this day knows how lonely I felt that night.

That night I made up my mind that home was no longer a place for me, and I would get away, but when the party returned home, I felt better and not caring to leave my sister alone, I tried to forget, but I was not allowed to forget for long, as some weeks afterwards my sister decided to get married.

Of this ceremony I was not informed, until the night before the wedding morning, and I don't think I should have been told then had it not been that I saw new dresses and things coming into the house, and I asked what was happening, and was told by my sister that she was being married on the following morning.

This gave me a great shock, as I was not particularly struck with my sister's young man, (who by the way was a bandsman in the salvation army) and I said I would not go to the church, but my sister started to cry, and eventually I was persuaded to go to the wedding.

The next morning, after getting to know what time the ceremony would take place, I set off to work as usual, as I did not want to lose any money over the affair.

Well, the wedding took place and I very well remember coming home and getting dressed, and then taking my place beside the driver on the cab, of course there was no room for me inside, and when we got to the church (Hunslet Parish Church) I sat as far at the back as I could get.

Of course being Salvationists it was a very quiet do, and after tea I went off to the local fairground to enjoy myself until bedtime, and my life went on until I got so dissatisfied with everything and everybody, that I decided to clear away from what was home, so one Sunday morning I and a mate of mine made up our minds to set off for Scarborough, and try our luck.

I run away from Home

Never shall I forget the morning in the middle of November, when I left home in my wild passion, as I thought for some years, but how sadly my hopes were shattered.

Getting up at 5:30am, it was with a very heavy heart that I prepared a cup of tea for myself, and got ready for work, as my sister and her husband thought, they were still in bed.

I drank my tea, but could not eat, and, after a little meditation, as to whether to keep my promise to my pal, or not, I decide that I would go on with the adventure, so going into the cellar, I purloined a loaf of bread, and went out of the house.

Many times, going down the street, I stopped to look back at the old home, that I thought I had been driven out of. Not could I get my mind at rest until I came to the appointed place of meeting, and there sure enough, was my mate, waiting for me.

That morning will remain in my memory for all times.

We set off as fast as our young legs would go, and as we thought, enjoying the freedom of the country, but we had not gone many miles, before we began to feel tired and weary, so we sat down to have some bread to eat, because both of us had forgotten to bring any butter or tea, we had to eat dry bread, and later on we begged some water.

Starting off again we managed to arrive at Tadcaster, but not wanting to stay at any town, we went straight on towards York.

A few miles further along the road we came to a house, which by the aroma issuing henceforth, there was a good meal being cooked for some lucky individual, so I plucked up all my courage, and knocked at the door, and asked for something to eat, as we were very hungry, but I had to go back to my pal, broken hearted, because I had such a bullying at the hands of a big man, and then kicked down the garden walk.

We started off again, and as it got dark very early, my mate soon began to wish he was at home again, but I was determined to carry on, and I had to get vexed to stop him crying, but eventually, I gave in to him, and we gathered some wood, and never dreaming that we were breaking the law, we lit a fire on the roadside.

As the flames sprang up, we soon began to feel a little warmer and comfortable, but this small happiness was short lived, as soon after this, a policeman came along and asked what we were doing.

I can't very well remember what I said to him, but I told him some story or other, and whether he believed me or not, I do not know, but after a while he seemed to be satisfied, or else he did not want to take us in, and he then directed us on our way to York.

We Arrive at York

Starting off again, footsore and weary we arrived at York, as near as I can recollect about 9pm, and wandering around, not knowing where we were going to sleep, we came to the river bridge, and sat on a seat, and it must have been close to midnight when we heard a noise coming out of the dark, but it was a rather nice soft noise, and so far as I can remember now, neither of us was afraid.

The man with the noise came nearer to us, and began to question us as to what we were doing there at that time of night.

I, being always the spokesman for both of us, started to tell him a tale about having no parents, and that we had no home.

We afterwards learned that he was a detective, and after a bit of talk, he told us to go with him, and he led the way to the police station.

Arriving at the police station, we were again put through another examination, by who appeared to be a superintendent, but I shall never forget the kindness of those policemen, because they made us some cocoa, and one of them gave us bread and butter and cake, for which we were most thankful.

After finishing our meal, we were conducted to a cell, and over some blankets we were very soon asleep. It did not seem long before we were awakened, and brought before another sergeant, who questioned us again, and after further talking, we decided we would join the army as drummer boys.

The tale I told seemed to be very satisfactory, anyway, we were then escorted to the Salvation Army home where they gave us some cocoa and thick slices of bread and jam, which we enjoyed very much.

When we had done eating, and got outside, we found to our relief, that the man in blue had left us, so we made our way to the barracks, my mind fully made up, that I was to become a soldier, but owing to a fault in the fitness of my mate, I was again doomed to disappointment.

Arriving at the barracks, I made enquiries from the sentry, as to how I could become a drummer boy, and he called for a corporal, who conducted us to the recruiting room.

There we were asked our errand and having convinced the sergeant that we were orphans, he gave us some more food, and told us to remain beside the fire, until the doctor arrived.

When that officer arrived, we had of course to strip, to be put through our paces, and I was pleased to hear him say I was a fine made boy, and I passed with flying colours.

My pal came next, and I was ever so delighted when he had nearly completed the first, but when it came to a (liss) of the feet, I was horrified to hear the doctors say that my mate was flat footed, and therefore could not join.

Now came the time when I was to fight between my pal, and my ambition to become a soldier. The officer and the sergeant tried all they could to persuade me to sign the papers, but after a long while, I said I would not leave my mate, and don't think there could possibly have been a more abject or disappointed boy in the whole world than I was when we went out of that barrack gate.

We walked down the road, not speaking word to each other for some considerable time, until we came to the Minster, then sitting down for a time, we began to talk again, and to try and forget the incident at the barracks. Whilst sitting there in the November sun, I happened to notice a tram going by which was bound for Scarborough, and realising that our object in the first place, was to go to that fishing town, I said we would get along on the road.

We journeyed along for some miles, until we were within a couple of miles of Malton, and then feeling a little discouraged, we made up our minds to go back to York, which we did, arriving in the minster city long after nightfall.

We had had nothing to eat since breakfast in the Salvation Army, with the exception of a turnip each, which I am afraid we stole out of a field, and then being hungry, cold and tired, I may wager there was not two more disconsolate kids in England.

We had been tramping about the streets for some time, when I saw a man smoking a cigarette, and I went up to him and asked him if he would give me the tab end, but judge to my amazement, when I found it was the police officer who had taken us in the night before.

This officer was very nice to us and after a good talking too, he took us to the workhouse, where we were given a bath and some food and then put to bed.

The next morning we were given some work to do, to pay for our nights lodgings.

My task was at a pump, but what I was pumping I don't know to this day, as I could not see any water or anything coming out of the pump, and to my enquiries, I was told I was pumping wind into the bedroom of the workhouse staff.

Eventually the time came when we were to set free, 12 midday, and after being given a meal, we set off again, not knowing where we were going to.

During our walk, we came to a bridge with a river underneath, and a path, so I asked a passer by, where that led to, we were told the path led to Goole, and not having heard of that place before, we decided to go there. Trudging along the riverside we got to Goole about 4 o'clock in the afternoon, and walking round and round, until at last, I think I must have been desperate, as I went up to a man and asked for some money.

The tale I told must have appealed to that man, as after a few words he gave me three coppers, so of course I was once more a wealthy boy.

I did not keep the wealth very long, because not very far away, I saw a light in a shop window, and going up to the shop we found it was a bread shop, and bread and such things being cheap in those days, we got, as we thought, a very good supply for threepence, and with this food held very tightly we set again to find a spot where we could have a feed.

After this we again made our way along a canal bank, an as, by now it was getting quite dark, we had not the faintest idea where we were going to, when suddenly we heard some music, and then we arrived at some steps which led over a bridge.

Crossing over the bridge, we saw some big boys, one of which was playing a melodeon, and as I was a very fair singer in those days, having been in the church choir, I began to sing the tunes which were being played.

By and by we saw the doors of the houses opening, and elderly people looking out to see who was singing, and after quite a long time, which I suppose was the time when every body should be in bed, we again found ourselves alone on the road, but richer to the extent of about sixpence, which my singing had earned, and seeing the inhabitants putting out their lamps, we thought it the better way to take the canal path again as we did not know in what village we were in, nor where the road would take us to, and we did not want to run into any more police.

So making our way again, we came to the path and went merrily, but cold, along our way.

It must have been getting very late then, as we both felt very tired, and at last we came to a big hay stack in a field, and I thought what a nice warm place we could make by pulling out the hay, and making a hole big enough for both of us to get into.

This task being done, we got into the hay, and had a good two hours sleep, when we woke up very cold, and never dreaming that big rats had been running over us in our sleep.

We set off to walk again alongside of the river, but had not proceeded far, when we heard the swish of water, and looking round, saw to our wonder, a boat coming along, and lucky for us, it was quite close to the side, and I said to my pal that we would jump aboard, and have a ride as far as we could.

We had been on the boat about half an hour, or as near as I can guess, when the barge woman put in an appearance, and asked what we were doing there. Of course, I told her we were very tired and cold, and had nowhere to sleep, so she turned very kind and gave us a pot of chocolate each, and some bread and meat.

But this ride was to end very soon, as a little further on we came to some locks, which the boat had to go through, and then we learned that we should have to get off, as the boats were not allowed to carry passengers.

So, again with heavy hearts, we again took to the path, and about six o'clock in the morning, although it was still very dark, and not a soul about, except our two selfs, we thought we would try another sleep.

With this in our minds, we climbed over a wall into a field and huddled together, we tried to sleep until it got daylight.

Not knowing where we were at this time, we started off again, and soon came to a town which we learned was Castleford.

I had still some coppers in my pocket, so we purchased a pot of tea each, and some bread, and feeling absolutely done, we enquired our way and how far it was to Leeds. Then off we went on our way and about mid-day we arrived in Pontefract, where we were told we had a straight walk of eleven and a half miles to Leeds. So we made up our minds, to make our way back home.

When we did get back into Leeds, we began to realise how foolish we had been, and we were both afraid to go to our homes, and we eventually decided to go to the Salvation Army in the hope that someone would take us home.

We had not been there very long before my sister's husband came along, and took me home, where I was very glad to get a talk and a hot meal and to bed.

The days passed away very well after this, and I got a job as an errand boy for a firm of cleaners of clothing, and I had to take the parcels to the houses of the owner, and many times I had long distances to go.

This was not too bad in summer, but I well remember one day in the depth of winter, I was sent with some parcels, and it appeared to me to be ever so far.

I delivered my parcels with the exception of one, and being half starved and hungry, I sat down by the roadside and cried.

I remained in this position for some time, until a man came along and asked what was the matter, and when I told him I was crying because I was cold, he was rather sympathetic but then he called me all the soft heads, and all kind of things, and then he volunteered to take me to the house where the parcel had to go. I was very thankful for this, as by now it was getting dark, and I did not quite know where I was, and after I had given the parcel up, I went back to the shop and then was very pleased to hear the mistress say that I could go home, as there were no more parcels for that day, and I was very glad to get home and get beside a warm fire.

I stayed at this work for several weeks, until I thought I was too big for an errand lad, and I wanted some other kind of work to do.

Days passed by and I was beginning to feel downhearted, when one night I went home feeling fed up, and on arriving in the house, I saw a young man sitting there, whom I knew was a miner, and he said he wanted me to go and see the manager of the pit, as he wanted a boy for a hurrier.

This was glorious news to me, and I was ready in next to no time, but I was persuaded to have some tea, before I went out, but that did not take long. I interviewed (with) the deputy foreman, and he being quite satisfied with me, he told me I could start down the pit on the following Monday.

Oh, what a day that was for me. Set up with brand new clogs, and I am sure we tried to make as much noise as we possibly could when we were walking through the streets at five o'clock in the morning.

After a very long walk, we came to the pit head, but I must say I felt a bit nervous, when I saw what we had to go down the pit in, but one of the older men got hold of me and said, when we got into the cage, "now my lad, get hold of the bar and close your eyes".

When the cage was loaded, and all was ready, the collier put one arm round me, and said we were going to start, and I felt an upwards movement, and then a sudden drop of several feet, although it seemed to me to be miles, then we went steadily down until we came to the bottom. There was no gas in this pit, so of course we used naked lights for our works, and I found then, that we were issued with our lamps at the pit bottom.

I may say that no prouder lad was born, than I was, when I was given my lamp and candle, and told off to follow a big fellow, who was a hewer, and I was told he would be my boss.

We set off to what was known as our hole, that is the coal face where we were to work, and what a long way we had to walk, sometimes bending so low that we were nearly creeping, and although there was plenty of corves or tubs passing us on our endless rope, I was told that we were not allowed to ride in them, as it was considered dangerous.

We eventually arrived at the coalface, then I was told I could have my snack, whilst the hewer got a tub of coal ready for me to take to the pass by.

This work did not take long, and I was soon on my first journey. I felt a little afraid going away into the dark, with only a small lamp at the front of the corve, but I soon got used to the darkness and before we had done for the day, I thought I was a proper miner, and I was greatly surprised, when my boss said it was time to knock off, and that when he had got another load for me, we would go off together, as the next shift would then be coming in.

After a while my load was ready, and off we went towards the pit mouth, where we were very soon hauled up to daylight, and how glad I was to see the light of day again.

Things went on very well until the following Saturday, when something happened, which made me afraid of the pit.

I was on a journey from the coal face, when my light went out, and not having a match with me, I had to trust to the rails bringing me into the right direction.

I had gone quite a long way, when I found to my dismay I had run into a dead end, and then I knew I was lost, and I could not think what to do. So I kept on shouting and hollering as loud as I could, in the hope that someone would hear me. And after what seemed to me to be hours, I was much relieved to hear my shouts answered. But it had been a terrible time for me, as I knew the pit closed at 12 noon Saturday, and I was afraid that I should not be found, and so I should remain down the pit by myself until the following Monday morning, when the first shift would be coming down. Of course, I did not know then that a roll of men and boys down the pit was taken, when the last man or boy was brought to the top.

I did not stay very long at the pit after this, as I was sometimes scared and got too afraid to go down, and I wanted a more open life, and a few days afterwards, I and another lad a bit younger than myself, set off on my second journey to Scarborough, determined this time to get onto a fishing smack.

As I had been on the road before, as I have previously explained, I was more familiar with things in general, and consequently, it was much easier than when I first made the journey, and we arrived at York quite early in the first day.

On this occasion I had a few shillings in my pocket and a bit more sense, so we did not stay very long in York, and after having something to eat, we set off on our way again, and as it was in the summer months, we could stop and rest for intervals, and walk on again without being too tired.

It must have been getting rather late and growing dark, before we decided to have a sleep, so we crawled into the hedge bottom, and were very soon asleep. We had quite a good rest, and when we awoke the next morning, the sun was shining brightly and it was very warm, and after eating some bread which I had got at York, we went off again, and very soon we came to a town, which I afterwards learnt was Malton, where we were able to buy a pot of tea for each of us.

Feeling refreshed after our meal, we did not tarry, as I was very anxious to get onto a fishing smack as soon as I possibly could, so we pushed on, and about mid-day we arrived at the port of Scarborough.

Making our way to the fish pier, I soon got in touch with some boys who were playing about, and being of a friendly disposition, I was quite at home amongst them, and we were happy playing about on the sands, until our stomachs told us it was time to have something to eat. So we went off to a tea stall and had some tea and the remains of the bread.

After this, we had nothing to do but hang about the boats, and see if we could get picked up by some man or other. We walked about for quite a long time, till at last we got brave, I suppose by not seeing anyone about, and we jumped on to a smack which was quite close to the pier.

We had not been on the boat very long before we were accosted by a big man, who I understand now, must have been the watchman, and of course we had to explain what we were doing there.

The man was very fatherly towards us, and after we had told our tale, he gave us some good advice, and told us some terrible tales of the sea, that my mate turned soft, and began to cry, saying he wanted to go back home.

The fisherman gave us some food, and packed us up some ship's biscuits, and told us to go on shore, which we did. I tried very hard to persuade my companion to try to get on a ship, but he would not, and not caring to part company, we set off back again towards Leeds.

I will not dwell on our return walk, but I think it took us somewhere about a week to do the journey.

After this I made up my mind to try and settle down to work and to stay at home, but my wish for a roaming life was too strong, and I tried to get into the navy, but here again I was doomed to disappointment.

Instead of going to work one morning, I waited about in town until I could see a recruiting officer, and when that person put in an appearance, and I had explained my errand, he took me into a public house to test me. I passed the test with flying colours, and thinking that everything was in my favour, I was told to hang about a little while and my papers would be made out, and then all I would have to do would be to pass the doctor, and as I felt in the perfect pink of condition I was naturally in my element, as I thought nothing could now stop me from going to sea, but, oh, what a disappointment, when the medical man said I was quite fit, (he also said) I should be obliged to get a written permission from my Guardian, (who at that time was my sister), before I could be taken on.

After this setback I wander(ed) around the town until the shambles opened, because I used to go there and help the butchers to kill the beasts and sheep, and in this manner I whiled away the time until it was time to go home and get tea ready for my sister who was working, and I thought I should be able to get hold of my birth certificate before she came home. Well, I hunted round, and opened drawer after drawer, but could not find my paper anywhere, when who should come in but my sister, who had finished work earlier than was usual, and of course she wanted to know what I was doing looking through the drawers.

Now I thought I was in a bit of a pickle, and after a while I determined to own up and I told my sister I wanted my birth certificate and also her permission to join the navy as I wished to go to sea.

That naturally caused a scene and of course she did not want my tea, but sat crying for some considerable time, and I feeling a bit fed up, I went out to play about until she had got over it. When at last I went into the house all was quiet, and I thought it the better plan to get off to bed, and leave my business until the morning.

Next morning I was up with the lark, hoping to get the document I wanted, also my sister's permission to go away.

But again I was doomed to disappointment as I got neither permission nor anything else, so I went to work, and tried to think of something else and a safe way of travelling abroad without so much walking about and sleeping out at night.

I got a decent job at my old trade as a boot riveter, and remained at the firm for some time, until I got the roamers feeling again, and got very unsettled, and so one morning instead of going off to work, I wandered about the town until the recruiting office opened, and at the time when I thought I should have a chance of seeing the sargeant, I made my way to the place in very good hopes of going away.

I did not wait very long before the fellow in seardes (?) tunic put in an appearance, and to him I told my tale.

He was very decent up to a point, but he would not believe me when I said I was eighteen years old, but I eventually persuaded him to fix me up.

Of course the first thing was to strip all off and stand before him, and I was pronounced as very physically fit, but, oh, horrors when he measured my height, it was to tell me I was about half an inch under the standard. I think it was then I began to cry, and the sergeant seeing my utter disappointment, took a little pity on me, and gave me sixpence, and told me to come back again on the following morning, and he would see what could be done. After that I played about all the day until it was time to go home as if I was coming home from work. I said nothing to anyone about my day off, and next morning I was up like a shot, hoping it would be the last time I should sleep in that bed for some time to come. I made my way to the recruiting office in quite good spirits, and arrived there a good half hour before the appointed time.

When the man in red did arrive, he eyed me up and down, and seeing I was determined to go, he measured me again, and then said he could take me into the militia, until I got to the standard height. I was delighted with what he said and then I was told to be back again at a certain time, when he would take me to the station and put me on the train for my destination.

When I came back at the time, the sergeant came with me to the station, and having got my ticket he gave me a shilling (which I afterwards learnt was the King's Shilling), and put me on the train, telling me to change at York.

Up to this time I did not know where I was going to, and being alone in the carriage, I pulled out my ticket and found out 201 was bound for Richmond in Yorkshire, where I arrived somewhere about eight o'clock at night. Now was the time I began to feel a bit lonely, I suppose by being alone and in a strange place. I did not know what to do, but as it was rather cold and dark, I pulled myself together and enquired my way to the barracks.

My way was pointed out to me, and off I went, feeling a bit downhearted, but at last I came to my future home, and felt much better when I came to the gate, and saw a soldier marching up and down.

This, I learned, was the sentry, and I told him what my errand was, and he directed me to what I know now was the guard room.

I went into the room, showing my papers, then I was sent to another room in the barracks, where about half a dozen more lads like myself were.

I was given some rather good cocoa, and bread and butter, and then talking amongst us I learnt that these lads were recruits like myself. I was then given some blankets and it was not long before I turned in, wondering what would be said at the house when I did not turn up for my tea.

It was quite a long time before I could tempt sleep that night, and next morning I felt worse than ever, but after a good wash and a breakfast I began to fall in with the other fellows, who did not seem to care.

After a while a soldier with two stripes on his arm came into the room and told us all to follow him, and took us all to be medically examined and then we were taken to a large stores and given our uniforms, and by job did I feel proud when I first put it on, little thinking what I should have to go through before I took it off for good.

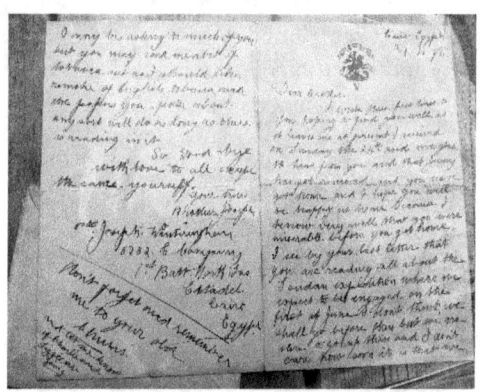

Joseph Winteringham's letter from Egypt, dated 1898

Horse rider in South Africa, presumed to be Joseph Winteringham

My Adventures in German South West Africa Transport - in the year 1905 - by Joseph Winteringham

Transcribed from his notebook by his granddaughter Jane Cooper (née Winteringham)

In the month of January 1905 I resided in Pretoria South Africa, and as the times were very bad I thought I would have a little change of air. At the time and for some months past (many) were recruited for South West Africa as transport riders, and of course I made up my mind to see this country where some many were at war (with the Herero and the Namaqua). At the end of January, after I had made everything square, I determined of getting away as soon as I possibly could. So making my way to Comdt. Schordir's office in Schreman I entered my name on the long list of men about to leave their home for the land of war. Although war had been raging in South Africa for the last three years it would appear that these men had not been satisfied, but it was not war which drove them away from their native land, it was simply go away or starve as work was very hard to get at that time in South Africa.

Well enough of South Africa. Now before leaving Pretoria I made up my mind not to see the place (again). So after disposing of my little property I was ready to make a start for the new country. So on Friday morning, the 3rd February, I boarded the 7.30(am) train bound for Germiston. On my arrival at the latter station I had to wait till 10.40pm for the through Cape train so with a few Pounds in my purse I wended my way to the town to look round and pass my time away as comfortably as I possibly could. So entering the first hotel I called for breakfast as I was rather hungry. After this meal I walked round until mid day and feeling a little weary I entered a bar to rest, ordering a glass of beer. I picked up a paper and prepared for a comfortable read. And so the day past until 10.40(pm) rolled round and up to time. I went rolling away as fast as two engines could carry me towards Cape Town after most enjoyable journey on Monday morning, 6th February. Now, not having been in Cape Town for over 6 years I could not imagine where to go so wandering along I turned along Bree St. and put up at the Albany House until such times as I could get a steamer for G.S.W.[3] Africa. After dining I and a few chums walked round the town and seeing nothing to interest us, returned to the hotel to await dinner which was served up at 12.30. Then after a game of cards we went for a

---

[3] Publisher's Note: German South West

little nap in our respective rooms and so time passed away until dinner time rolled round on the following day (Tuesday). After this meal we wended our way to the docks to see our ship which was to carry us away from the land of gold as South Africa is called. Having heard that a mail boat was about to leave that afternoon for England we decided to see her departure wishing at the same time we were going to board her but our fate lay in another direction. After watching the Galician[4] sailing away we retraced our steps to Bree St. with heavy hearts. That night I received orders to embark on the following day so after breakfast on the Wednesday morning I took myself down to my ship which was being loaded up with donkeys for the country we were going to. At 10.30am, I walked up the gangway of the General as the ship was called and from that time and also for several days after I served under the German flag. That night we slept on board but did not sail until the following morning when at 9.10am the anchors were draw up and shortly there after we left Cape Town behind. With a calm sea and good steam we soon passed Robin Island and lost sight of Table Mountain and got well out to sea. Nothing worth notice passed until the 11th (Saturday) when our journey was made a

---

[4] Publisher's note: it is the Galician SS (1900-1914), managed by the Union-Castle Line, which owned the greatest fleet ever to serve South Africa. It was renamed Glenart Castle HMHS at the start of World War 1

little livelier by watching Whales and Porpoises swimming about the boat. That same morning we saw a coolie buried at sea then everything went well until about 8 o'clock Sunday morning our destination was sighted and about an hour afterwards we sailed into Swakopmund harbour. Now this port is not like our English ports as there are no docks to unload cargoes and all unloading was of course to be done by barges and tugs so thinking that we should have plenty of work to get all the donkeys off (600) we commenced at once to unload and very good sport it was. Three o' clock in the afternoon saw us finished for that day not because it was Sunday but because the sea was too rough to allow any more unloading to be done. Monday at about 12 midday saw the General an empty ship again as we were thinking of landing about 1.00pm and were ordered to the raft close by the ship's side. But we did not land at that time we lay tossing about for some hours before a tug came to draw us in land, and in the meantime, we had time to dine once more on board the General. Well fortunately all the tugs were not in use and about 7 o'clock that evening we set off for shore but another delay was waiting for us and that was the tug which came for us was too small for the journey and therefore we got another tossing about until a larger tug came and about 8pm we accidentally found ourselves jumping on to what is know as the quay and after being searched by the customs we we're allowed to proceed on our way to the tents which were some distance off. That night we slept in what is called a tent but I should give it another name. Any how next morning we awoke to find ourselves full of little red pimples and scratches caused by the company which styled our bed mates. These were good mates to sleep with but the only fault is they won't allow you to sleep. Tuesday and Wednesday we were engaged in the kraals[5] inoculating oxen for going up country and all went smoothly along until Thursday morning when I was ordered to make my first trek up country.

---

[5] Publisher's note: "enclosure for cattle or other livestock" in afrikaans

Portrait of Joseph Winteringham in military uniform (before 1914)

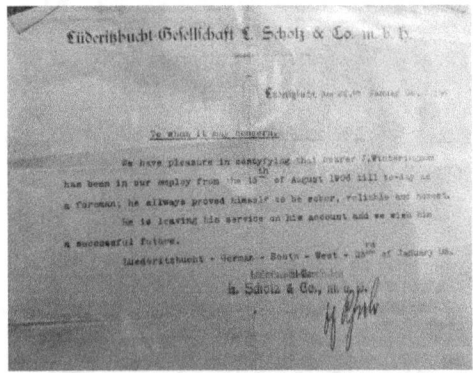
Reference letter from Luderitzbucht L. Scholz & Co.

My First Trek in Deutches Sud West Afrika in 1905

Time passed away until my time was up when I entrained at Swakopmund at 1.45pm on Thursday the 16th of February with about 400 sheep and on the following morning we arrived at a small station called Ausskus[6] at 6.00am after kraaling and counting our sheep we prepared breakfast which did not take long as it was only bully and biscuits and then after a little sleep we watered our stock ready for a good night trek across country to Karibib which was 27 kilometres. We trekked that night until between 8 or 9 o'clock and as the sheep retired we gave them a rest. But unfortunately we were not allowed to sleep as we had to keep a close watch as (the Herero and the Namaqua) were supposed to be in the kopjes[7] close by. Anyway I did manage to put in 2 1/2 hours in my blanket until daybreak, next morning we were away again for another few hours before the sun made it too warm to trek and about 9am we rested our stock in the veld[8] again ready for another trek in the cool of the evening. About 4pm we started again and trekked on until about 7pm when we halted again on the veld for the night. I

---

[6] Publisher's note: today's Usakos
[7] Publisher'snote: pl. for a small hill or mound, especially on the African veld
[8] Publisher's note: "open, uncultivated country or grassland in southern Africa"; also spelled *veldt*

was not so bad off this night as I was one of the lucky ones and I had a good night's rest. As we had no water all that day you can imagine our feelings, and I did not sleep very well until 3 or 4 o'clock. In the morning we were cheered up by hearing oxen wagons coming along the road, and we knew they had water with them and when they did come up to us I was about the first there after the sentry and I had a damn good fill of water then I lay down quite at ease until about 5.30am when we made another start for Karibib where we arrived about 9.00am on the Sunday morning the 19th February. Here we received our food and rum and tobacco for the week and after having a good pipe of bacca and then we had a good clean up and then a little sleep until 4pm when we trekked again for Halbricht Brummon (?) or Hasserstetts (?) about 4 kilometres from Karibib. About 6pm whilst trekking on a ford between hills a very severe thunder storm overtook us and of course as therein was in our faces the sheep refused to walk any further so we abandoned the hope of reaching the water place until the storm had subsided. Well at the time of this storm I was only clothed with a thin suit of clothes as it was the summer time and the covering for my head (had) been a cap. Well the storm had carried on for some time when I was taken with a giddy feeling and rolled to abash where I tried to take cover but was instantly struck by what I thought to be lightning and I knew no more until I found myself on Monday in the hospital at Karibib where I stayed until the following Monday when I asked the doctor to allow me to proceed to join my transport again. But not (being) able to find my transport I was given a ticket to proceed by rail to Okahandja. On my arrival at the last mentioned place it was about 4.30pm and never being in the village before I of course did not know where to go so making my away across to a big tent I found to my delight some watch fellows who of course I knew to be transport men so putting down my kit I made my way to a hotel and after strolling around for some time I accidentally dropped across a young fellow who had come from Pretoria with me and after a chat I found out he was with a loose mule transport making their way to Windhuk[9] so I made up my mind to join them if possible so after seeing the conductor I was disappointed to hear he had a full number of men. That night my friend invited me to have some tea with him and of course I did stay and being some way from the tent where my kit was I decided on sleeping with my friend. Next morning whilst quite dark I was awakened by hearing the men saddling up to trek so I rolled out of my blanket and I very luckily heard that one of the men was sick, so going to the conductor I asked to go up to Windhuk with that transport and so of course being one man short and having

---

[9] Publisher's note: today's Windhoek

brought my kit from the tent I left Okahandja about 5.30am on the road to Windhuk, a distance of 78 1/2 Kilometres or about 60 English miles. We travelled along at a good speed until about midday we arrived at a small station on the line called Teufelsbach where we found to our dismay that there was not sufficient water for our 200 miles so of course we could not stop there as we had intended to do and turned our mules and we made our way back to the main road and coming to a dry river bed we halted our stock a(nd) digging a hole for ourselves we prepared our midday meal cooking bacon or spick[10] on the embers of the fire. After resting ourselves for a little while we start again for the next station called Otjihawera where we arrived quite safe at about 6pm having trekked that day about 44 kilometres and I can assure you we were well pleased to site that small station. Here again we unfortunately could not get any water for out stock so of course we left them in the kraal all night without water. After our meal we cast lots to see who should stand guard band being fortunate in getting the dogs watch (12 till 1) I was very soon under my blanket and I did not takes very long until I was asleep and I did not wake again until my mate shook me and told me it was 12 o'clock so of course up I jumped and with my rifle I walked around the kraal until 1 o'clock

---

[10] spick = a side of bacon

when I woke up another driver and I was soon in sleep again. Next morning being Sunday we had not far to trek as we decided upon not going into Windhuk and making an early start we arrived at what's called Brakwater about 9am where our mules had a plentiful supply of water and then turned out to graze. Here we remained all day enjoying a good sleep under the shady trees and when night came on I got the 11 to 1 watch. Next morning making a wary start we trekked the 15 1/2 Km and arrived in that glorious city the capital of DSW Africa, Windhuk, at about 10.30am and after handing over our stock we made ready to travel back to Swakopmund by the first train in the morning.

After a good sound sleep in the station yard we awoke the next morning to find our train quite ready to carry us away. At six o'clock we left Windhuk and steamed slowly away to Okahandja at which place we arrived at about 2.00 pm. Now as there was a war in the country trains did not travel at night time so we had to make the best of it and stay the night in Okahandja. About 3.30 we handed in our saddles and rifles and went to draw our pay after which we had a drop of beer then we had our dinner. Next morning we boarded the 6.00 am train and arrived that same day in Karibib, and the evening following about 11.00pm we arrived in that dismal hole Swakopmund. Nothing of interest occurred here excepting we had the daily work as before such (as) inoculating oxen. Well being sick and tired of this dirty place I set about to look for another transport and fortunately I got a transport of oxen which where going that day to Windhuk and being taken on by (Condr) Harding I got my mule ready and about 4.00 pm on the 14th March 1905 I left Swakopmund gain determined to stay away until my time was up but fate would have that I would stay away longer than I thought as shall relate further on in these pages. That night we camped at a small station called Honidas (?) and next day we made a very good trek of about 36 kilometres and we kept on in this way day and night until we arrived at a small station called Worlt River Humrd[11](?) or in English "dry river bed" and it may well be called by this name as there was never any water in the river except by digging for it. At this place we intended to stop until our cattle were rested but we were destined to stay longer than we had intended as our cattle were taken with that disease called "rinderpest" and lung sickness and a telegram came that night saying we were to remain there until further orders. Of course we then started to rig up a kind of tirsac (?) for ourselves. Here we remained for two months and nine days during which time we

---

[11] Arrived here March 21st 1905

lost nearly all our mules and horses and also a good number of oxen.

Everything passed pleasantly away at this station until on the 2nd of June 1905 we trekked again on our way to Karibib were we arrived about 9.00 am on the 8th June. Here again we received rations and such things as we required and then trekked on to Halbrect Brummen (?) where we rested our cattle for a couple of days and then trekked again to Ojimakoko (?). This trek (was) taking us two days and on the third day we arrived at the station where we found a good supply of water and also good grazing for our oxen. There we remained until the 17th June when our oxen were inspected and found unfit to travel and we were ordered to remain another 21 days. Now at this time having been on the veldt for over 3 months we were very short of money, and I and another driver took the train to Windhuk to get some money and some necessary articles. On Monday afternoon about 2.30 we arrived in Windhuk. Hearing that we could not draw any money that day we started off for the tent where a lot more drivers were staying and here we remained for two days before we could get any money and on the Wednesday afternoon I and my friend drew 100 (German) Marks or five English Pounds each. When we received this money of course we must have a drink and proceeded to the first hotel to have a drink which I may here mention was the means of my misfortune in DSW Africa.

Joseph Winteringham's war medals

Joseph Winteringham on horse in military uniform

A Letter

Mrs C. Miller
Elandrhewel
Karlsdorf

Laid in Windhuk Bezirksaamt from 11th October 1905 to 8th Dec 05

8th Dec brought up for trial and remanded until 16th January 1906

Appeared on trial again and was once more remanded until 27th Feby 06

On 26th Feby received summons postponing 27th February and to appear on 18th April 06.

On the 18 April I was in hospital at Okahandja but my case proceeded without my being there and I was proved not guilty before the high court. Therefore I was discharged on my return to Windhuk.

Commenced for L. Scholtz Co (L Bucht Co) 15th August 06

Went into Lazarette 27th September 06 and came out 9th October 06

Commenced work again for same firm 10th October 06.

Joseph Winteringham and his battalion (undated; ca. WW1))

Costume party with fellow soldiers (undated)

Letters of Joseph Winteringham

Transcribed by his Granddaughter, Jane Cooper (née Winteringham) and his Great-grandson David Tripepi

Letter #1 written during the Anglo-Egyptian conquest of Sudan

Sunday March 20th 1898

Cairo

Dear Brother

Just a few lines to let you know we arrived safely at Cairo. I have not much to say only that we are under orders to advance to the front under General Kitchener. They are going to try and take Khartoum so we must be prepared for and after that we shall come out of it all safely. I must tell you that we got tossed about a lot in the Bay of Biscay but I am glad to say that I got here all safe without either sickness or anything else.

There are one or two famous things here either the Pyramaids and the Mosques. Then there are the natives running about with no clothing, only just a bit of cloth around their waist.

I think that is all this as I have not seen much to tell you about yet. I will have more to say next time if all go well. Don't forget to remember to all your chums. So good-bye till we meet again.

I am sending you our Gazette which will tell you where and how we are stationed. I will try and send it every month.

Will you try and send me a few things if you can afford it.

From your loving Brother
Private Joseph Winteringham
5252 (?) Company
1st Battalion Northumberland Fusiliers
Citadel Barracks
Cairo
Egypt

Don't forget to give Jimmy the letter inside

Letter #2 written during the Anglo-Egyptian conquest of Sudan

Cairo, Egypt

27 - 4 -1898

Dear Brother

I write these few lines to you hoping to find you well. As it leaves me at present I received on Sunday the 24th and was glad to hear from you and that Jimmy has got removed and you have got home and I hope you will be happy at home because I know very well that you were miserable before you got home.

I see by your last letter that you are reading all about the Soudan expedition where we are expected to be engaged on the first of June. I don't think we shall go before then but we are sure to go up then and I don't care how soon it is that we go up because I have not come out here for nothing you can bet and if I go up I shall soon get the Egyptian medal and star to decorate my breast with and not only that but I shall be very proud to say when I come home again that I went through a war before I was nineteen years old and there is not many can say that I know. There is rumours going about here that as soon as this affair is over we shall remove to Newcastle or Bermuda in the West Indies which is a pleasant station and is not quite so hot as this place.

I am send(ing) you last month's Gazette and in (it) you will see that I have marked out two or three things about Egypt such as the barracks where we are stationed and the big mosque which I mentioned in my last letter. Then you will see the natives and how they are dressed. I am getting alright with the officers and everybody else just now but there is some when they see you getting on well they try to put on you so when this does occur you have to do your best and give a kicking if possible and if you can't do it with your hands you have to use something else you will know what I mean by that.

I think that is all this time only that I am writing to Hannah and Will as you asked me to do. Tell Lizzie to write as I have forgot her address. Wishing her many returns for her birthday.

I may be asking too much of you but you may send me a bit of tobacco out as I should like (the) smoke of English tobacco and the papers you spoke about. Any sort will do as long as there is reading in it.

So good-bye with love to all except the same (?) yourself

Your true
Brother Joseph
Private Joseph Winteringham
5252 (?) Company
1st Battalion Northumberland Fusiliers
Citadel Barracks
Cairo
Egypt

Don't forget and remember me to your old chums.
And let me know if Charlie and Lizzie are going.

Writings of Joseph Winteringham

Transcribed by his Granddaughter, Jane Cooper (née Winteringham)

Untitled

Joseph Winteringham is my name

Pretoria is my dwelling place

South Africa is my station

Christ is my salvation

When I am dead and gone and all my bones are rotten

This little book will tell my name when I am quite forgotten

I have a heart and one so long it went from me and it flew to you

You have my heart pray treat it well

You know my name and where I dwell

And if you treat it kind and true I will not ask it back from you

But if you treat it with disdain you will kindly rerun it back again.

Dr. Peter sat on a marble stone

Twas to God he made his moans.

Peter Peter what makes you shake

My Lord my God the toothache
Peter rise and follow me
And the toothache shall part from thee
Whoever shall keep this in memory and write it for my sake
Shall never be troubled with the toothache.

Under the Bamboo Tree[12]

Down in the jungle lived a maid
Of royal blood though dusky shade
A marked impression once she made
Upon a Zulu from Matoboolo
On every morning he would be
Down underneath a bamboo tree
awaiting there his love to see
and then to her he did sing

Chorus:

If you like me as I like you
and we like both the same
I'd like to say this very day
I'd like to change your name
Cause I love you and love you true
And if you love me
One live as two two live as one
Under the bamboo tree

II

And in this singled Jungled way
He wooed the maiden every day
by singing what he had to say

---

[12] Publisher's Note: this is Joseph's transcription from memory of a popular 1902 song by the same name, written by Cole and Johnson Bros

One day he seized her very gently squeezed her
And then beneath that bamboo green
He begged her to become his queen
The dusky maiden blushed unsure
And joined him in his song
Refrain

III

This story strange but true
Is so often told in Matoboo
Of how this Zulu tried to woo
His jungle lady in tropic shady
Although this scene was miles away
Right here at home is done today
You'll hear some Zulu every day
Gush out this soft refrain
Refrain

Napoleon's Farewell to Paris[13]

Farewell though splendid citadel
Metropolis called Paris
Where phebus every morning
Shouts forth refulgent beams
Where flora's bright aura advancing
From the horizon
With radiant lights adorning tho
your shining streams
at eve when senator does retire
and the ocean glides like fire
The universe admires our ……
dire in store.
commanding flora's fragrance
the fertile fields to decorate.
To illuminate the royal Corsican
on the French shore.

my name is Napoleon Buonaparte
the conquerer of nations
I have banished German legends,

---

[13] Publisher's Note: this is Joseph's transcription from memory of a popular English ballad from 18th century which became a common street tune after 1893, both in Britain and across the British Empire

and drove kings fron their throne.
I have conquered dukes, earls and splendid congregations
though they have banished me to St. Helena's Isles.
Like Hannibal I crossed the Alps
The burning sands, and rocky cliffs
over Russian hills, through frost and snow
I still the laurel wore
Now I am in a desert isle
rats would devils affright.

But I hope to shine in armours bright
through Europe once more.
They say the cause of my downfall
was the parting from my consort
to wed the Germans daughter.
Which grieved my heart full sore
but the female frame I nil shall blame.
She did me …. defame
she saw my sword in battle flame
and did me adore
how I severely felt the rod
for wedding with the house of God
coin and gold images in thousands away I tore (?)

I stole Malta's golden gate
I did works of Gods disgrace
but I adore the cross and crucifix,
and now my pennants set.
My golden eagles were pulled down
by Wellingtons allayed army
my troops all in disorder could
no longer stand the field.
It was cold that afternoon
on 18th day of June
my reinforcements proved traitors
which caused me to yield
I am an allayed rash
with fire and sword I made them smoke.
I have conquered Dutch and Dane
both Portugese and Prussians
Like Joshua, Alexander or Ceaser of the rat (?)

And to the south of Africa
and the atlantic ocean.
To view the wild emotions,
and the flowings of the tide
bold boom the royal crown of imperial promotions
from the French throne of glory.

To see those willows glide
I stood the power
liberties caused me to maintain
thousands I have slain
and covered Their gaze.
I never fled without revenge
nor to an allayed army cringed
so now my sword is in the sheath
and Paris is no more.

The Sailor & the Jew

A German Jew in Portsmouth town carried a peep show up and down. That is a box whose work (?) contains mountain valleys rivers and plains cities and lakes much more of course than Troy capacious wooden horse which are Jew to each beholder resemble Atlas whose broad shoulder they support this earthly falls lands trees houses men and all. He stopped we're he saw a crowd set down his box and then allowed to all tat past without sensation proclaimed this general invitation vill you see this fine show shows all de cities on de Rhine de duke de raton (?) fines fine garden and much oder rare clings of course you know and many's a gaping country town that drove his teams to town pulled a half penny to see the strange film of Germany one fool of course brought many more. Moses took half penny's by the score his pockets wide began to swell and thus were all succeeded well but how little mortals ken when chance they meet a friend or foe a jolly tar in rigging knot striped cotton trousers and jacket new and new felt hat which seemed to say some ship has been paid off today came near the box our active Jew begged he would stop and take a view avast you lazy dog cries jack and careless passers by. Vahat's dat you call me me lazy dog de lor take care me glad to see you kick mine box and din kick me de lor take care, upon mine vord me silver shilling I'll afford to see you kick my show to pieces do man who break a potter's dishes oh, jack thinking it no great sin to earn a shilling in a minute smashed and all that's in it. But o how soon jack's blissful stare for Fruinphant (?) must evaporate see armed with laws gigantic might a policeman appears in sight holds up that baton so formed able to petrify the lawless rebel through Kerrick Hill and Sandy Row he quickly takes poor jack in tow. The vanished vector hangs his head and mob bore witness to the fact and swore that here the box was cracked and the Jew declared upon his word one silver shilling he afford if jack would smash his box. The justice in his morning gown and velvet nightcap with a frown calls Neptune off springs to his presence and tells him he would like to know what was the meaning of the smashing up of this man show so said the sailor all I know is that this man desired to see his gingerbread stove in and I thinking no great sin smashed his box and all was in it as for the truth sir if you doubt it ask all these good folk here about it. Then the mob who witness to the fact and swore that ere the box was cracked and the Jew declared upon his word one silver shilling he'd afford if jack would smash the box and jack they had done it neatly. The justice turned his awful look on Moses with clever rebuke. Friend I perceive though are in the wrong whilst next your angry hold your tongue it is plainly proved that you were willing begone and pay the man his shilling.

On the Banks of the Wabash[14]

As I wandered around my Indiana homestead
In the distance looms the woodlands clear and cool
Twas there I spent my happy childhood
Where I first learnt my lessons at natures school
But there's one thing missing in the picture
Without her face it seems incomplete
For I long to see my mother in the doorway
As she stood there years ago her boy to greet.
It is many years that I did wander
Arm in arm with Nelly by my side
It was there that I tried to tell her how I loved her
And I asked her if she be my loving bride
For the moon shines fair tonight upon the Wabash
Through the fields comes the breath of new mown hay
Through the sycamore the candle lights are gleaming
On the banks of the Wabash far away.

---

[14] Publisher's Note: this is Joseph's transcription from memory of a popular 1897 song by the same name, written by American songwriter Paul Dresser

Recipe for Eno's Fruit Salts

2oz of Epsom salts

2oz citrate of magnesia

2oz cream of tartar

2oz Tartaric acid

2oz carbonate soda

2 tablespoons caster sugar

Mix all together and keep tightly corked up.

Lambak

1d Swallow oil

1d Elle (?) oil

1d vaseline

1d bees wax

Colds & Mouthwash

1d Borling Magnesia

1d best salts

1d oil of peppermint

Scald in 5 pints of water.

Timeline of Joseph Winteringham's life

Tracked by his Granddaughter, Jane Cooper (née Winteringham)

- 20th May 1879 – Born in Boroughbridge, Yorkshire, UK
- 1881 – Recorded in the census as living in New Street, Boroughbridge, with Mother Hannah and 5 siblings
- 21st July 1887 – Joseph's older brother William is sent to Grimsby as an apprentice on a fishing smack
- 22nd September 1897 – Attested for the Northumberland Fusiliers in Leeds, UK, as Private 5252 for 1st Battalion
- 20th March 1898 – Stationed at barracks in Cairo, Egypt
- 30th May 1903 – Discharged from 2nd Battalion Northumberland Fusiliers in Bloemfontein in today's South Africa; attained rank of Sergeant
- 15th August 1906 to 23rd January 1908 – Worked as Foreman for Luderitzbucht L. Scholz and Co. in today's Namibia

- 20th February 1909 – Married to Eliza Harrison at St Michael's Church in Buslingthorpe, UK
- 19th April 1914 – Re-enlisted in the Northumberland Fusiliers for the 2nd battalion as Company Sergeant Major (CSM) of the N. 4 Company, Regimental No. 8488
- 15th June 1916 - mentioned in General Haig's dispatch, published in the London Gazette, for his service in France
- 17th July 1917 - transferred to a sick convoy with neurasthenia[15] from 12th battalion
- 1917 to 1920 – Training battalion at 13 Camp Durrington, near Stonehenge
- 3rd January 1920 – Transferred to the army reserve
- 15th April 1932 – Died of pneumonia and buried in the UK at Leeds General Cemetery, grave No. 7735; occupation on record was Commissionaire

---

[15] nervous exhaustion, used to describe shell shock

Portrait of Joseph Winteringham

www.ingramcontent.com/pod-product-compliance
Lightning Source LLC
Chambersburg PA
CBHW071504070526
44578CB00001B/441